I0111982

Conflict

RESOLUTION
REFLECTIONS

Phill C. Akinwale

Conflict Resolution Reflections

Published by Praizion Media

P.O. Box 22241, Mesa, AZ 85277

E-mail: info@praizion.com

www.praizion.com

Author: Phill C. Akinwale

Editor: Catherine Van Herrin

Copyright © 2013 Phill C. Akinwale

All rights reserved. No part of this publication may be reproduced, transmitted in any form or by any means including but not limited to electronic, recording, manual, mechanical, recording, photograph, photocopy, or stored in any retrieval system, without the prior written permission of the publisher.

The author and publisher accept no liability, losses or damages of any kind caused or alleged to be caused directly or indirectly by this publication.

Printed in the United States of America

Table of Contents

CONFLICT

Conflict! A steaming cauldron of rage,

Run and hide,

But it lurks on the next page.

Conflict is a potential for schism,

But deep within,

Lies a potential for giving.

Giving one's perspective,

Adding to the pie,

A conglomeration of ideas,

Both yours and mine.

Don't run or hide,

Just persist in the storm,

And at the end of controlled conflict,

A brand new idea will be formed.

PROLOGUE

When Barney Gladd actually started to think about conflict – honest, true conflict, he was amazed at how much conflict he had experienced in his life, starting in childhood. Childish squabbles in the schoolyard, fights with boys and girls in school, and arguments all through college. His early days at his first professional job were plagued with conflict – he and his "mean ol' boss Mindy" (as he called her), could never agree. In fact, he only lasted three weeks in that position. It was an absolute nightmare from hell for him. Mindy was always riding him hard, handing him more and more work and complaining about his performance, though he tried as hard as he could.

His second job was a bit better: he had a Theory Y manager who gave him free reign and believed that Barney gave his best, but his third job required him to work remotely.

Even though he never met his team, Barney noticed that they didn't get along very well. One was rather passive-aggressive, not saying much on the phone or during web conferences, but he unleashed his venom via email. His other colleagues seemed to be preoccupied with their own worlds, not allowing him entrance or, sometimes, not even noticing he was there when he needed something. This behavior continued until a team-building initiative was implemented, which helped bridge the gaps somewhat, but it was really just a temporary Band-Aid, and nothing was ever done to build team cohesiveness until he left the company.

Barney's conflict resolution and management skills had never been put up to a real test – no "trial by fire" type of test that would challenge him in every way. Sure, he had a few arguments here and there, but no career-type conflict that would register on the charts.

As he embarked upon his fourth high-powered job, he couldn't help but wonder what it held in store for him. He always came across as someone who could inspire, motivate or teach – someone who could make things happen. However, his skills had yet to be put to the test.

He had moved his family from the United States to Dublin to take on the managerial position of an organization in a state of flux. Staff at all levels had been recruited over a relatively short period, and managers were traveling all over

Europe to learn how their company's regional hubs operated. They completed speedy handovers and ultimately shut down those outposts. There were so many balls in the air, so many egocentric, larger-than-life personalities, and such a propensity for chaos, there was a very real danger that everything would come crashing down. This organization really needed someone special, someone talented, to pull it all together while keeping opposing stakeholders at ease. The company needed a good mediator.

THE MEETING

The project sponsor looked over the project team with a sneer, thumped a finger on the table one last time, and announced: "We will have world-class customer service by March 30th, or there will be big trouble for each of you!

"You call yourself a project team, but you're a joke, a scientific experiment gone wrong! You're a cross between senseless beasts and imbeciles. I demand world-class customer service on 3/30, or you will find yourselves in big trouble!" With that, he stormed out of the status meeting.

Barney composed himself and said, "Okay, we have four weeks until the deadline. Let's figure out what we can slap together in that time."

"We can all rewrite our resumes," Sharon, a systems analyst, quipped with a smile that faded when no one laughed.

"That's been your attitude all along," snapped Bill, a customer service department manager. "This project is going to kill us. You and your geek buddies will go on to some new project and leave us with a stinking mess. Your software doesn't give us even half of what we need, and my people can't use it!"

"Well, you can blame yourself for that," the IT analyst answered. "You've changed the requirements each week. What do you expect when you do that and then send less than a third of your department to training?"

"There's nothing wrong with our training program," Jill, the human resources representative, piped in. "Attendance has been a bit low, but we're going to make the training more enjoyable this week."

"Oh, I'm glad to hear that," Bill scoffed. "Maybe your trainers could have spent some time learning the application instead of making things fun. Can they even use a PC?"

Penny, the purchasing rep, responded. "It's not our fault that the PCs were late in arriving. No one told us about the order until a week ago."

Barney watched his new colleagues end the discussion in a flurry of disagreements, raised voices, verbal abuse and non-productive conflict.

From that moment on, Barney realized he would need some tremendous mediation and conflict resolution skills to make his decisions matter. It was evident that he would be faced with conflict management and leadership challenges.

Barney went home depressed about what he felt were his lack of conflict management skills. He preferred not to have any type of conflict whatsoever, and in the past, he had resorted to smoothing-over and avoidance strategies to manage conflict. But now he was smack-dab in the middle of it, and there was no apparent escape. He needed to do something fast to develop some skills or hone in on his near-inept ones.

He searched frantically through his collection of books and self-help materials that he had spent so much on but hardly ever read. He had almost given up when he stumbled across a book that he immediately began to eagerly devour. He turned the first page, ready to soak up all its contents, and encountered a quote…

"Whenever you're in conflict with someone, there is one factor that can make the difference between damaging your relationship and deepening it. That factor is attitude."
William James

Chapter 1: Conflict!

What is conflict?

When you think about the word "conflict," what comes to your mind? Do you think of two people in a physical fight, or enduring a battle of wills? How about two people in a power tussle for a top position? Or some form of irritation about someone's perspective, work ethics, views or opinions?

Perhaps you imagine each person trying to put his will, wants, needs, ideas and objectives above someone else's.

When subtle or even overt conflicts arise between people, they may not be verbal; some of these conflicts may emerge due to an annoyance about work approaches or perspectives, and some arise due to irritation between people. Sometimes differences between people cause conflict, such as when one party believes that his view, approach to life, or approach to work is better than someone else's.

This kind of "unspoken" conflict is often just as jarring and frustrating as a screaming match. Consider the word "will," as in an individual's "will" to do or believe in something. Your will is strong, right? But when you remove the "will" factor from the conflict, what happens? You may not see visual conflict, but there could very well be internal conflict, which can be corrosive. It can build up in someone physically and fester. Where do you think the phrase, "I'm burning up inside with anger!" comes from?

But consider this another way: If we remove people's ability to exert their will over others, does conflict remain? Sadly, the answer is yes; conflict will remain, because internal conflict is powerful and usually builds up slowly. The other person may not even know you're feeling a sense of strong conflict toward him!

Again, conflict is a very powerful tool, and it can be used to pacify problems or further damage situations between people. When someone feels conflict, say between family members, friends, or even close relationships, those relationships are likely to suffer – unless you use conflict in a productive manner. Yes, it can be done!

Statistics show that you experience the most conflict with those whom you are around the most; however, you do not experience much, if any, conflict among those you are not around on a regular basis. For example, there's no conflict with the guy at the post office or the cashier at the grocery store. You probably enjoy a reserved but distinct cordiality.

How about kids? Why does conflict arise between parents and children? Is it a battle of wills?

The anatomy of conflict arises from a battle of wills in which each person tries to have his way, and because this is an impossible scenario, conflict occurs.

"Effective conflict resolution is a goldmine of opportunities waiting to be won by the best conflict miners"
Phill C. Akinwale

Chapter 2: Defining Conflict

What is conflict management and conflict resolution?

Conflict management is the effective management of any form of conflict to arrive at a final resolution – one that satisfies the best intentions of both individuals and results in a "win" for both parties. This is also true within an organization or business unit – the key word about conflict management is just that – management. It means each person has to willingly manage the conflict to arrive at a final decision at which both people, organizations, the family, the mother and child, or the business unit win. Conflict does not always move right into arguments, fights and bitterness.

Now, let's consider another question: What do you regard as the results of conflict management? Many images or ideas may come to mind, like that bitterness, or, even worse, things like envy, worry, disharmony, illness, anger, wrath or danger.

When you thought about the results of conflict management, did you think of that "win-win" situation? Most people don't. The word "conflict" does, after all, carry a connotation of tension, fighting, stress or other upsets. But the word "management" connotes an idea of togetherness, structure and stability. So when you put those two words together, you're literally "stabilizing stress," right? That means conflict resolution can glean great results, magnificent ideas, best-in-class processes, success, agreements and a tremendous output of goodwill.

Amazing, isn't it? But if only calm and peace existed, how would a person or organization feel challenged? We need conflict – it can be a very positive thing, because without it, we'd never reap its results, which can bring about the best in an organization or challenge people's ideas by stirring up the synergies of people.

However, there is one thing about conflict that people often forget, and it is essential: conflict must be controlled, because it is inevitable. If you put one person in a certain environment and ask for their help in a certain work area, that sounds pretty straight-ahead, and it usually is. But if you bring another person in and ask him to do the same thing, expect some conflict!

Since antiquity, men have always been in conflict with others – war is not a new concept.

So, though you certainly don't need to declare war between cubicles or draw a line across the office to "take sides," conflict is inevitable in a project management environment or in any organization, because when you put two people together, they will at some point have different ideas, exert those ideas by virtue of their will, and create conflict. Maybe they have different ideas about what works or they argue over the scarcity of resources. Maybe their scheduling priorities and personal work styles conflict. Maybe one person shivers in a sweater and the other is comfortable wearing short sleeves and light clothing because of differing temperature needs. You can put the kindest, most compassionate, caring, loving, understanding people together in a work environment, and despite all that kindness and compassion, they will encounter conflict, and then they will express it! It doesn't matter how compatible two human beings seem to be – the propensity for conflict is always there.

But conflict doesn't have anything to do with people being the friendliest or best of friends – conflict is just part of life. Friends experience conflict just as enemies do. Families *don't* always live happily ever after! They go through what can feel like intolerable conflict – but it doesn't have to feel that way if you learn to manage it.

"Family is conflict and it's something that we all relate to."

Bill Cosby

Chapter 3: Team Dynamics

"**T**hink about how teams develop.

Consider the five stages of team development and how they are a perfect example of how and why conflict ensues. You may be surprised at how quickly you can move through these stages, or how you sometimes can literally "skip" a few with teams you have worked with successfully on previous projects.

The Five Stages of Team Development

1. Forming

2. Storming

3. Norming

4. Performing

5. Adjourning

In the *forming* stage, the team members meet for the first time, and everyone tries to be on their best behavior.

In the second stage, *storming*, the team begins to address the project, including technical decisions, the project management approach, and so on. At this point, if the team members do not collaborate or if even one person has a closed mind and is not open to different ideas and perspectives, the environment can become counterproductive.

This occurs because conflict has arisen, and at this point, you can either make or break your team and your team project. When conflict arises, it becomes one of the biggest barriers to teamwork, and that's why conflict is so important to manage. So, at this point, it is essential that the team creates an agreement that includes everyone's ideas about how to approach the project.

If the team is successful and clears the storming stage, it then moves to the *norming* stage, where the team members begin to work together and adjust their work habits and behaviors to support the team as a whole – as one unit. In fact, one of the major goals of conflict management is to leave your personal agenda behind and learn to act for the greater good of the team.

After this stage, you move into the *performing* stage, where, at its best, the team functions as a well-organized, inter-dependent unit. Team members depend on each other's ideas and can agree to disagree. This means they are armed to work through issues smoothly and effectively. Certainly, issues will continue to arise, but ideally, the team will work through them in a mature, effective way. That is one of the goals in conflict management.

Next, in the *adjourning* stage, the team completes the work and moves on from the project with a sense of accomplishment.

Here's the good news about the five stages of team development: any team that has successfully gone through these first few stages in one project will very quickly be able to cut to the chase and reap the rewards by skipping some of the stages in future projects.

Now, these five stages are also known as Tuckman's Ladder, which is a group dynamic theory that states that though it's very common for these stages to occur in order, it's not uncommon for a team to get stuck on a particular stage or even slip back into an earlier stage. This means the team can move into the norming stage and then slip back into the storming stage. Teams that have worked together successfully can usually skip that stage, and that's good news.

To move effectively from the forming stage to the storming stage to the norming stage, the team must develop a deliberate, intentional approach to resolving conflict, and that means that the team must realize that conflict is not a bad thing – that they should embrace conflict, because within it, you will find the life blood of great ideas and refine them.

Sure, anyone can have great ideas, but without some push-and-pull and team-tussle, you won't have a well-tested, trial-by-fire, innovative solution. So, again, there is absolutely nothing wrong with conflict! It just depends on how you look at it!

"Peace is not absence of conflict, it is the ability to handle conflict

by peaceful means."

Ronald Reagan

Chapter 4: Good Conflict

Conflict is not bad!

Conflict is not a bad thing: it's simply inevitable. The source of conflict, especially in the work environment, revolves around work styles, resources and scheduling priorities. The only difference between "good" and "bad" conflict is your approach to it – your perspective.

Team ground rules, group norms, and solid project management, such as planning communication, defining roles, and helping people understand their value and the value of their project can *reduce* the amount of conflict. Successful conflict management always yields terrific results, like greater productivity, better working relationships and teamwork.

However, if conflict becomes a negative factor among team members, project leaders are responsible for resolving those differences.

If conflict escalates, project managers should step in if it begins to impede work or leads to an unsatisfactory performance or unacceptable customer deliverables.

Because you, as a project manager, cannot make up two people's minds, the best way to resolve conflict is to bring these two people together synergistically so that they can collaborate and realize that their inability to do so could put the entire project at stake. This is where the project manager can act as a mediator or arbitrator while listening to both viewpoints.

Now, obviously, if someone's viewpoint is to the detriment of the project or organization, you can't deem it acceptable, but if it's simply a matter of differences of opinion and work styles, project managers should step in and help resolve those.

Before they dive into conflict management, sometimes project managers or business leaders think, "Is it worth it? Is this worth moving to the conflict resolution process? Is this really a point of conflict? Should this kind of conflict be given any consideration?" If the answer to most or all of those questions is "no," it's always best to move along very quickly and simply bypass it.

Some issues are just not worth arguing about. There are some problems, usually miniscule, that would only be a disservice to staff and company time if moved over to conflict management. But, if this very tiny problem or issue escalates, then project managers and management staff, should help facilitate a satisfactory resolution by addressing the conflict as early as possible.

There are many different signs of conflict, and some are more subtle than others. For example, if people begin missing meetings or find reasons to leave the office early, those could be very big signs that they are experiencing conflict. If disruptive conflict arises, then you may have to resort to formal procedures such as disciplinary actions.

I've met several project managers who share a mindset that conflict management is something that functional managers or human resource managers should resolve. Nothing could be further from the truth! Though many project managers have varying ideas about how to resolve conflict, the ultimate success of the project falls very heavily on the project manager's *ability* to resolve conflict.

"Conflict is both an opportunity to lead and to be influenced towards a cause greater than the sum of two personal agendas."
Phill C. Akinwale

Chapter 5: Influencing Factors

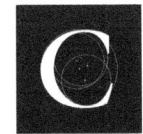

C onflict influencing factors – what about them, and what are they?

One factor is the relative importance of the conflict – as mentioned earlier, some issues just aren't worth pursuing. Another factor is whether the conflict could potentially affect a particular project or a deliverable service negatively.

That's always a cause for concern, because when your company's quality output is at stake or unsteady, customers will sense this, so take that to the conflict management table immediately.

And how about time pressure? Exactly what is at stake as far as time is concerned? If the conflict continues beyond one workday, consider whether that could that jeopardize the project or the deliverable. If the conflict continues for an entire week, that could easily put the company in a bad light. Don't let two major players on a project wreck your project just because they are unable to resolve conflict. Step in and take action – and fast.

The other factor that could influence conflict resolution is having a solid process that motivates everyone to resolve conflict on long- or short-term basis. How do you motivate people to resolve conflict? Put solid, ground rules in place, including consequences for being disruptive in the work place or while working with a team on a project.

Conflict ground rules and consequences for improper management of conflict situations should be clearly defined at an organizational or business unit level to be followed and understood by all.

"Difficulties are meant to rouse, not discourage. The human spirit is to grow strong by conflict."

William Ellery Channing

Chapter 6: Five Approaches for Resolving Conflict

Five general approaches for resolving conflict do exist, and here's where you can learn to apply them!

Each of these five general approaches has its place and specific use, and these are not given in any particular order: one or two might be frowned upon by certain individuals, but let's take a look:

Withdrawal or Avoidance

When someone leaves, withdraws, or uses other avoidance tactics to distance himself from conflict, this means that you will not be able to resolve the conflict for obvious reasons – the party has left the building! If and when this happens, it's usually due to a person's natural but very non-confrontational personality. They just don't want to address the issue.

You'll also find others showing avoidance behavior due to lack of preparation – maybe someone does not have the facts, figures or the energy to deal with the conflict.

Others retreat because they distrust authority or are otherwise unable to work as a team, again, due to personality. If this is the case, third parties should be brought in to help resolve the conflict by arbitration or mediation.

Withdrawal on a permanent basis is very dangerous to the project's success and the company, as well. It tears a hole in the group effort, and when the stakes are high, this can be disastrous on a company and customer level. It can also decrease the team's morale. When you retreat from conflict, you cut off your ability to add value to the equation, and you remove value from the business or organization.

In some instances, a complete withdrawal like this can be thwarted by keeping your mental antenna sharp and deflecting a conflict altogether, but if the person has already withdrawn, give him a chance to cool off so that temperaments remain steady. For example, you could approach the person privately and suggest that he take a break for a few hours and then re-engage later on in the day. Take this time to let the person voice his concerns and intents and thank him for his insight. But sometimes, you might need a few days instead of hours. It depends on your situation, and everyone is different. Make it clear that you intend to resume the discussion, but do not leave the impression that you feel defeated.

Smoothing

The next conflict resolution approach is smoothing, or accommodating. This is the stage at which you strongly emphasize how and where you agree with the team member instead of emphasizing where you disagree. One person may have to concede, or "agree to disagree" and shake hands to maintain team harmony. It may not completely resolve the conflict, but it shows that you accept the other person's viewpoint and emphasizes the places where you are in agreement. Steer clear of those issues on which you disagree – there's no time or use for that, because you have to keep moving ahead for the good of the project, the team and the company. Besides, usually, no further deliberation will change the person's viewpoint anyway! Don't use a negative tone; just be a professional and leave the areas of similarity on the table.

Compromise

Compromise, or reconciliation, occurs when you seek a solution that brings some degree of satisfaction to other team members to temporarily or partially resolve the conflict. Bear in mind, however, that this method usually doesn't completely resolve the conflict, but it does give people some form of relief.

Compromise is all about finding that middle-of-the-road spot where you can both co-exist. It's never a perfect scenario, but if there were such a thing in business, there would be no need for this book!

Compromise is also different from smoothing and accommodating in that you're not necessarily emphasizing the areas of agreement; instead, you are looking for a common point, a solution, with which you both can live.

Forcing

Well, forcing is exactly what it implies – it is quite frankly a very dangerous method of conflict resolution, and it's all about one person pushing his viewpoint at the expense of others. Often, this is a win-lose solution, and forcing is typically used through a power position to resolve what has become an emergency situation.

Some people abuse this type of conflict resolution by employing it too readily in non-emergency situations. However, if for some reason your team or your project has deteriorated to the point at which you must use this method (which you shouldn't, because you're a good project manager), simply resolve the conflict with a very direct approach.

For example, if a company is about to tank, several decisions need to be made within 24 hours. These involve buying and selling decisions related to stocks, shares and other liquid means by which the company can reduce its assets, and only a CEO or another high-level associate can make these decisions. In times like these, there is no room for deliberation. That decision could be "forced" or "directed," depending on the emergency situation.

Collaborating

The next technique is collaborating, or problem-solving. This is one of the most beneficial approaches to conflict resolution because it incorporates multiple viewpoints from those involved, and it offers various insights on different perspectives.

Have you ever tried to put a finger in front of your face and close one eye, then look at your finger and close the other eye and look at your finger? If you keep doing this, what happens? Your finger appears to "move" because you have two viewpoints – your left and right eyes. This is just a simple illustration to further show how viewpoints can shift and change, as well as influence or determine a person's perspective toward a problem. So, to get a well-rounded view of a conflict situation, both parties must be willing to look at it from the other's perspective, and collaborating, or problem-solving, involves those multiple viewpoints.

You could be dealing with two viewpoints or 10. The number doesn't matter – the point is that trying to get into other people's shoes, so to speak, to see their point of view, can often be a dizzying thing!

To effectively resolve conflict through collaborating, it's very important that all parties adopt a cooperative attitude and keep an open dialogue. Gossip, malicious backstabbing or fighting, and speaking behind others' backs should never be allowed. To really open up the dialogue, sit down and look at the conflict and decide what to do about it jointly, from two or more viewpoints.

"Creativity comes from a

conflict of ideas."

Donatella Versace

Chapter 7: Equip Yourself

E quip yourself with key skills! But which skills?

When a businessperson tries to resolve conflict, certain key skills come in handy. So let's discuss the skills that a project manager needs to effectively resolve conflicts.

The first skill is essential – no project manager can do without it, and it is the skill of leadership.

Leadership

Paraphrasing the words of John C. Maxwell, "Leadership is all about influence; nothing more, nothing less." It means being able to influence people toward a common goal and enabling them to work as a team. It is the ability to get things done through others.

You can spot a good project manager by how he leads his team: he has great leadership skills and can easily influence the team positively. It's about leadership through influence, or by example. It's teaching others how to lead by example.

Another way to spot a good project manager or business leader is to encounter a team that has gone through conflict resolution successfully. The project manager must interact with his peers, subordinates and superiors on such a level that each person trusts and can put their confidence in the project manager. Good project managers also inspire others, who will often emulate them or learn through being mentored by them. It's always important for leaders to influence their teams, and that only comes from setting a good example.

A good leader must also have a team-building mindset. He must be ready to help team members in the middle of a conflict and stay the course. He must possess insight related to the individual team members and know how to steer them in the right direction. He must recognize when some team members need extra training. He must encourage things like trips or outings to help boost morale, if it applies to his project. He must be able to "see into" the team and decipher what it needs to move forward, toward the common goal.

What happens after a project manager or business leader successfully builds a team? Smart leaders look for positive outcomes like mutual trust, a high quality of information exchange, more effective decision-making, and stellar project management. For team building to work, executive management needs to lend its support and use company initiative to move the team forward. Show your team that you believe in the power of team building, and you will have a team with a dramatically reduced level of conflict.

A particular manager of mine once said, "You guys always have conflict; you always seem to be in arguments.

You need to resolve this. I'm going to give you both my credit cards to go out and talk about your problems."

It worked. We were a little surprised, but his actions enabled and empowered us to resolve our own conflict. He led by example, but also by subtle management, when letting us solve the problem ourselves.

Be an Inspiration

If you can't get motivated, you're likely not inspired.

Inspiration is more long-lasting than just feeling temporarily motivated. Think about it: Have you ever seen a leader or project manager inspire a person or team out of their self-limiting mindset to greater heights in their professional or personal lives, and with lasting results? Consider how invaluable that is! In the same vein, when you can inspire two team members in the middle of conflict to rethink, reconsider or change their "me-focused" mindset and be "we-focused," that ability is huge when it comes to resolving conflict.

Be a Great Communicator

Of course, communication *must* be on this list! It should go without saying, but the sad fact is that many managers and project managers do not communicate well, or at all!

Communicating is not just about being able to speak well or hold a conversation. It's also very much about being able to listen before speaking, as in "active listening," which simply means the person in question is not thinking about what the other person might say next or what he's going to say next – it means he's there, in the moment, and truly listening to the other person. This is really the only way to arrive at a mutual understanding of the issues at hand, and it's an indispensable characteristic for project managers. They not only deal with conflict, but also discussions that revolve around give-or-take or push-or-pull agendas, and so forth.

Active listeners know when to be passive; they know how to conduct a "held-back" approach to speaking and a more active approach to listening.

Also, the good project manager puts his team first, especially during a potential conflict. The best approach is to say, "What's going on? Tell me about it," and let the person begin the discussion. It's what I call the "you go first" scenario, which puts the person's or team members' viewpoints front and center. It elevates their mood, which increases their morale, because they feel that their opinions and viewpoints matter. Then, all the project manager has to do is lead those people to an effective resolution. Never be the judge – always be the arbitrator!

Be an Influencer

The next skill, the ability to influence people, is really just another word for leadership – it's about getting people to cooperate, and it's all about the project manager being able to maintain a flexible, interpersonal style and adapt to the audience.

Different mannerisms and ways of communicating affect people's ability to be influenced. This skill is tantamount to a project manager or business leader's success and his team's success. You have to be able to converse with several types of people from several educational, cultural and/or ethnic backgrounds. If you can gain the confidence of everyone in your company or on your team, no matter where they came from or when or how, you're more than halfway there.

Be Decisive

Decision-making means being able to solve problems by deciding what to do, implementing it, and how to react in a timely fashion. It's all about being able to make a decision before the decision makes itself; it's about taking control and ensuring your stance is sound and that you are fully informed.

Be Culturally Aware

As I mentioned earlier, cultural awareness is a very important skill, because it directly affects how we speak to and treat those different from ourselves. We should also be culturally aware to better understand the project environment and to understand the dynamic between different backgrounds, such as the topic of diversity, and comprehend the expectations or mindsets of the people involved in a project.

One of the most difficult things to do is skillfully use cultural situations to the best advantage of the project and capitalize on those cultural differences. The project manager needs to create an environment of trust, and he must believe in it to then create a win-win environment so that people will feel free to open up and discuss differences.

The best way to manage cultural diversity is by understanding the different team members as individuals, and using great communication planning based on what you know about their background and culture.

Negotiate

Negotiating is all about leading the team to success. Contrary to what many people think, it's not about a one-party win – it's about both parties winning, and when negotiation is done well, both parties go away feeling happy and content, because they are able to live with the final decision.

Again, the most vital asset in negotiation is being able to attentively listen and effectively communicate. In one of the exercises in my negotiating training, we discovered that those who asked questions and listen attentively often walk away with a larger negotiating piece of the pie. The more you actively listen, the greater the chances of you finding satisfaction from the negotiation, and that should include both parties.

Build Trust

The ability to build trust with the team comes from your track record that you've built up in the organization, and it comes from the ability to cooperate and problem-solve.

Team members need to see what you have contributed and demonstrated as a leader. They learn this by observing your trustworthiness. In the words of John C. Maxwell, "Trust is like currency in the leader's pocket, with it they are solvent, and without it they are bankrupt." So, to be solvent, you need to be trustworthy and have developed a dependable trust brand over a long period of time.

Coach

The final skill is coaching, which is not about telling people what to do, but helping people realize and recognize their potential through empowerment, choice, decision and development.

Coaching is about guiding people toward their maximum potential, not telling or pushing them toward it, but really helping them discover their true potential. "How do you feel?" "What are you going to do about it?" "What are your next steps?" are typical coaching questions. Rather than telling people what to do, a good coach guides individuals toward their solutions or decisions. And those are big skills in every project manager's world – they must be effective conflict resolvers.

"I don't know a single person in life that doesn't have conflict."

Joaquin Phoenix

Chapter 8: Be a Resolver

More things can always be done to improve your skills when you find yourself in conflict situations.

As project managers, it's part of your job to effectively close and settle conflicts – partly because this helps guide your team and make your business prosper. Good project managers also learn lessons from every conflict and should always be ready to take on a mediator role.

In fact, many times, project managers find themselves in the middle of a conflict situation before they even realize it! It takes a super mediator to be able to think on one's feet, out of the proverbial box, and shell out the skills your team needs. To be a super mediator, you need to be willing to put yourself out there, and if any of the parties involved in the mediation are not willing, the conflict will remain unresolved.

I also believe companies should have formal training in conflict management or conflict resolution to eliminate the possibility of guesswork. Your team looks to you for guidance; they depend on you, so make sure you're prepared to take charge and diffuse the tension on your team.

In addition, I believe project managers should have team performance agreements or ground rules in which conflict management is discussed and benchmarks are made regarding how to resolve conflict.

Also, when acting as a mediator, it is very important that we don't offer personal advice. We should never let our private lives and beliefs interfere in our business lives. Once those lines blur, you'll stir up a lot of unnecessary confusion, so make sure you nail that coaching ability and guide people toward a final conflict resolution.

I also believe that every company should have an in-house conflict management program. That way, everyone is on the same page, training together, which eliminates a lot of miscommunication. Plus, any form of education is always a good thing, and when your team becomes better at resolving conflict, they will often be able to eliminate conflict on their own. Remember – everyone is working toward the same goal – to make the company more profitable. Why? Because when the company profits, top management profits, and then they pass those profits down to staff.

This is why it is very important that your team shares the same ideology – the same "win-win" mindset.

Also, consider how you look at the big picture of the conflict. Do you see through tunnel vision or through too many details to be able to step back and take everything in objectively? If so, you can change how you view company conflict – you can develop an integral vision to be able to see every point of view while also resolving the larger, more central problem.

It is also important to have a big-picture mindset or "systems thinking mindset" to identify how all the different pieces of the conflict puzzle relate to each other. An inquisitive approach is also your best bet when trying to resolve conflict, which means that as a mediator, you must ask the right questions to try to understand the context of the conflict.

Another thing that can really boost your efforts as a project manager is being careful to choose the right words and tone of voice when communicating with team members during a conflict. If you get upset or raise your voice, you can blow the top off of the entire project. Keep it cool under the collar and listen to yourself speak. Practice, if you have to, with friends or family members, or even in the mirror. So much of what you say is not *what* you say but *how* you say it – body language experts have always known this. How you speak and the words you choose can make or break even your best intentions.

In your approach to dialogue, remember that you must communicate in a give-and-take manner – no one respects a despot, so let the team members speak first to give them their turn on the "floor" first; you can approach the virtual podium after them. If your team disagrees with you and you feel you aren't getting anywhere, it's very tempting and a very natural reflex to become defensive in your words, tone of voice and body language. That is a big enemy of the collaborate mindset.

Also, try to bridge the gaps between yourself and your team by building an alliance that binds you together – you don't have to sit at the head of the conference table or grandstand in any way; they already know you're the boss!

Being innovative is another huge plus for successful project managers. When you're thinking creatively and putting your heads together, or brainstorming, for example, you're opening the channel to that burst of creative energy that leads to new and innovative ways of resolving conflict.

So, when resolving conflict, think of a common goal, be open, approachable and honest, never try to coerce or manipulate your team, never resort to verbal threats or defensive actions, and most of all, understand the team's needs. Group cohesiveness is a must, and it must also be established early on to avoid violent verbal outbursts that can wreak havoc and sustain irreparable damage on your project and your team.

"Conflict cannot survive without your participation."

Wayne Dyer

Chapter 9: Thoughts on Conflict

Let's review some conflict resolution thoughts from some of the finest minds in behavioral management today.

John C. Maxwell, thought leader and leadership guru, says, "It's very important for you to pick your battles as a leader – know when to push, know when to back off; it's very important to know when to let go."

When you let go at the right time, you will maximize your chances of gaining a win in a conflict situation. But how will you know when to let go? What are the signs?

First, try to spend time with people who are different than you are, regardless of the work setting. The more time you spend with people who have different perspectives, ideas, cultures, and even religions, the more you'll be able to appreciate and understand how these people think and work. This means you'll be less inclined to rush to judgment.

Second, when it comes to mere matters of personal preference or personal taste, just keep moving. This is one of those miniscule things that are best left as they are. Save your energy for more important things that really matter. If you keep putting out petty little fires over something as shallow as personal preferences, you'll just go in endless circles and won't be available when a real conflict presents itself. You'll also wear yourself out!

Third, don't take yourself too seriously, and don't take things too personally! Someone once said, "At work, I take myself very seriously, and at home I am very casual." It's important that we know when to leave our egos at the door.

Another thing to keep in mind is that some conflict arises due to human suffering of some sort, and that's a completely different ball game. Someone on your team may be depressed or hurting, grieving over a personal loss, or dealing with untold personal or financial problems. If you don't know what that team member is going through, you will miss the root of the behavioral problem.

The only thing we know is what we know about ourselves, and when we can push or back off at the right time.

John C. Maxwell also talks about practicing the 101 principle: "When you get into a conflict situation, find that one percent that you agree on with the other party, find that one percent in the common ground no matter how small it is and then give it the hundred percent of your effort to emphasize it and to stress similarities in a particular area. Remember the best team doesn't always win; it's usually the team that gets along the best.

EPILOGUE

Barney snapped the book shut and looked over his notes. He resolved to make a difference in his new job as a problem-solver, mediator, go-getter and, most importantly, a change agent with a backbone.

Barney had energy in abundance. He had humor – he made 12- to-14-hour days bearable! He soon became known as "Dr. Diffuser" because he resolved all manner of conflict on the team. People even knew when he was in the building, because he had the ability to lift the mood of his subordinates – his loud laugh made people feel that, even through tired, bloodshot eyes, you could still have a laugh!

Barney was a courageous leader – he implemented change by looking at the bigger picture, and he truly seemed to believe in the need to do the best thing for the organization, rather than the best move for his own career. He had confidence and seemed to understand people – his staff, in particular. He could absorb enormous amounts of information, take on a lot of pressure, listen attentively, deal with an overbearing project sponsor, and protect his staff when necessary. He proved to be someone who knew his stuff and was happy to pass on his knowledge.

Barney managed to build a strong, consolidated customer support and finance function – a large team of 120 motivated, well-qualified staff, with good systems and processes, poised to support a growing organization.

On his wall was a plaque with the word *RESOLVE* engraved in large letters. "Resolve" was his code word for success – each letter stood for all good things – rethink, evolve, solve, open minded, love, victory, empower.

RESOLVE

R – RETREAT to RETHINK the other person's position and yours. Don't jump hastily to judgment or conclusions.

E – EVOLVE in your reasoning to see the bigger picture and the greater good and EVALUATE all options.

S - SOLVE the problem. Seek solutions that will result in a win for all involved parties. Think "solution," not "position." This means negotiating creatively and jointly coming up with ideas to resolve conflicts or issues.

O-OPEN-MINDED people are great innovators and problem-solvers. Be open-minded with no preconceived ideas, judgments or assumptions about how the conflict will turn out. Surrender your defenses and "conflict weapons," and don't be defensive when looking for a resolution.

L - LOVE your job, your company and your colleagues.

V - VICTORY is achieved in win-win outcomes. Endeavor to find a place where you both win.

E – EMPOWER involved parties when in conflict. Handling conflict correctly empowers involved parties to make the best decisions now and in the future.

www.ingramcontent.com/pod-product-compliance
Lightning Source LLC
LaVergne TN
LVHW011338080426
835513LV00006B/427